Other Works by Marie Palmer

The Gift of Will:
A Road to Forgiveness, A Passageway to the Divine

—**FIVE STAR REVIEW**—
Finding Love and Forgiveness after Trauma

This book tells the story of a woman who was born into, and raised up in, a cult then thrust as a teenager into the real world. It talks about the struggles she went through both in the cult and upon leaving, and her attempts to process what happened and move on. It's a book about overcoming and the power of forgiveness. It's an enlightening read and a powerful story.

In a Place Where I Find My Wings

A companion guide to Marie's memoir, *Wings* is a collection of affirmations finding forgiveness, and discovering self-love and divinity.

moments in
SLUMBER

The Other Side

In that long alley
On that road
To the other side,
I saw them dancing.
They had their lives.
They had their stride.

They didn't question,
"Who?"
Or,
"What?"
Or,
"Where?"
They always had
That certain flare.

I wondered often,
"Where I would go?"

Instead, I found grace
In a place unknown.
On the other side,
I am more
Than my soul
Will hide.

So, if you wonder,
"Where you will go?"
Take a deep breath.
Off you go!

The unknown will take you.
That it will.
The reaper will have
Her cup to fill.

All we know,
On that quest to find,
Is what we will find
On the other side.

Snake Girl

There was once a little girl,
With a poisonous stare.
She often asked me,
"Where was I there?"
I didn't know what to tell that gal.
I was always just her pal.
But in that poison in her hooves,
I saw a lioness dressed in woods.
She trampled on the days that await.
She did not care about times for fates.
When that girl with a poisonous stare,
Left me there,
I started to glare,
At the world unfair.
And in that treachery,
That she left behind,
Was the seed
That boggled my mind.
Was that girl
With the poisonous stare
Just me and myself
With a mind to spare?
So when you see
That snake girl there
Know that I
Still always care.

Dolphin Man

Hey, do you remember him?
That dolphin man?

I can't remember.
Just go there.
Maybe I will find him.

I laughed.
I can't even remember his name.

Oh, but baby, that's a shame.

Oh pray tell, is that dolphin man
Just a man that is made of sand?

And in that sand bites clearly see,
That wicked man of sand was me?

The dolphin does his tricks for sure.
Making believe that he was pure.

But in the ocean and wider space,
There is a sign for that dolphin's race.
In that cold and darkened womb,
Lies that good old dolphin's tomb.

So now in the blessed dolphin's curse,
I hurry off with my big purse.

So when you find the dolphin man,
Ask the ocean, "Is he made of sand?"

So, when he carries you off with your purse,
You will find yourself a little less cursed.

The Nothing Box

Off I go to it with glee!
I am, but I am not, really me.

Off I go to the darkness here.
I might even drink a beer.

My nothing world,
Oh come. Oh, come.

I promise I am not made of scum.

I will sit and drool over pretty girls,
And find a cup of sweetened swirl.

Oh, take me now,
To my box so rare.

You will barely
Find me there.

The Witch and Weeds

There in my garden I found her waiting.
The weeds, she pulled, were mighty satiating.

She dug and pulled to kill those weeds.
But oh, to me those weeds did please.

She hurried to make me a potion dear.
Only to find me in my tears.

Oh, that witch that pulled my weeds,
Caught me in my wickedest deeds.

And now that witch she knows my garden,
And I will long to drown in Sodom.

How did she know that I was there?
In that place so soft and rare.

When all I wanted was her seeds,
But she had picked my wicked weeds.

Pandora's Box

Mask it now.
Run and do.
Do it quickly,
I am Jew.

I am few.
I am mind.
Censor it quickly,
I am mine.

I am few.
I am weak.
I am all,
That is so bleak.

I am black.
I am white.
I am female.
I am plight.

Do not open,
The door to me.
I am sacred.
Censor please.

Why do open,

Pandora's box?
Oh, religion,
Save me lots.

I cannot even,
Remember my name.
The politician's,
Mine the same.

Oh, cover me up,
Pandora's box.
Censor me now,
With Satan's locks.

I cannot
Be exposed, you see.
What if they find me,
Covered in greed?

Cover me.
Cover me.
Mind of few,
I am not the Censor.
I am not the Jew.

All I want,
Is Pandora's box.
Opened now,

Free of Satan's locks.

So tell me now,
Wild wicked pen.
Am I alive?
Am I Zen?

What will you do,
With censored me?
Will you send me to prison?
Will you set me free?

If I tell you,
To censor me now,
Will you buy me,
A sacred cow?

And oh, by the gods,
I morn for me.
But only I,
Morn for thee.
So, I open me now,
With a crow bar still.
Aching now,
To know my will.

Will you censor me,
Quiet and true?

I am black.
I am few.

Will you tell me,
That times are fair?
Will you find me,
A woman's hair?

Oh, for that sacred,
Pandora's box.
Open me now!
Uncensored locks.

A Piece of Prose

There was a man naked as can be. Practically, he looked at me. With that rare stare, that melancholy sullen glare, he asked a question rare. "What do you think, or believe?" said he. I simply said, "I believe in me."

The Shallow Shore

Where do the waterfalls go?
Like your tears,
Down, to the deepest shore?
Where the fish can swim no more?

To the shallow water shore.

Shades of Gray

"Shades of gray!"
That's all I say.
"Shades of grey.
Rainbow Fey.
Hey!"
Shades of Gray.

The Killer Whip

"Oh!" Please, make sure it stays the same.
All black and dark,
Toward that main vein.

"Make for certain! It bears,
All the scars,
All the tears."

"I see!" You have missed a spot.
You found a different sacred lot.
You should just dig so hard, and true.
In that one place, where pain does brew.

Even though, "I know it tears,
I know you will not stop to care."
Even though the wound is deep,
In that one spot you love to keep.

"I will keep," my sacred horn.
"I will not leave," to mourn.
In the wound, "my soul will heal."
I will hold an arrow teal.

So! When you will come to wound,
I will find your heart and swoon.

"So!" My arrow pierces your heart.
That wound will fill with dark.
With that dark, "I will aid a lark."

The Beggar

She sat all day,
Waiting at bay,
For the simple sun to shine.

She crept at the stars.
She danced to the moon.

Her head exploded to mars.

She ached with pain.
She resented every vein.
She moved like a corroding lark.
Her head exploded with the stars.

She sat with her sign.
She tried not to whine.
The bitterness inside was dark.

She could not find a spark.

She waited for me.
I had sympathy.
I could bring her a nourished mark.

I asked her, her name.
She said she was insane.

I said, "No matter! You played the part."

Feverish she was from the start.

"What do you want?"
She said, "It's a front."
"You wouldn't help a girl like me."

I said, "But I can truly see!"

I said, "Anything you like."
She said, "Why the spite?"
I said, "The choice is yours to be."

"I cross the ocean seas."

She finally conceded.
She wouldn't have felt needed.
If her own greed killed her spark.

I found an ancient soul.

So! I asked her to choose.
She would only refuse.
I got her whatever I caught.

So! To the beggar,
To the silent peddler,

Who plays that solemn part,
I will not be played the fool.

I give you a gift.
I will choose, until you lift,
The powers that choice did impart.

All this in the world of school.
I will not be played a fool.

The Nameless Tomb in the Concrete Walls

She tried to help, and to be good enough for them.
Everything she did was true.
Her reputation was impeccable.
For all that she had been through, she was fresh and
new.

But then came the time for her to unwind.

All that she stood for flew.
They took her there with a camera to stare.
They placed her in a concrete tomb.

The Man with the Hair

He stood erect.
His eyes were on fire.
He used her as bait.
He wanted to light a fire.

He took what was his.
In that taking he left a scar.
But the hair that was left,
Was only for his bazar.
One day she cried
In that blackened and horrifying train.
What he left behind as he drove
Was that painful stain.
She screamed, and she cried,
Out of the screens on their fast mobile.
Until the wounded could breathe no more.
And the colors she could not feel.

Now, the voices outside
Could hear her pleading drain.
And the bleating of this lamb,
Her voice would not be contained.

Now in this wounded cry,
The others would once heal.
To maintain her voice so solemn,

The voices could not conceal.

Now that her plea was known,
The boy that took the bait.
Was confronted by their design,
A confession
Would be all that he would make.

To be with this monster,
Now, could never be.
To be a patsy
For the long-lost serenity.

A Silent Love's Whispering Dream

Her mouth was sweet,
But silent.
I thought about feeling.
It was all the same.
I held myself so quiet,
But love had called my name.

She stood there quietly looking,
Her eyes were endearing and fair.
I looked to see much deeper,
That she was even there.

She came just one bit closer,
I felt her still far away.
The kiss was sweet and silent,
Her lips moved sailing to bay.

I tried to touch a piece,
Of what she left behind.
All that was left,
Was the silence of her mind.

She asked me, without asking,
If I would take her away.
I asked her without asking,
If she would stay the same.

We felt the heated potion,
Of emotion here and beyond.
I tried to pretend to kiss her,
But my heart was way too fond.

She stood there in that moment,
Looking at what I would do.
I stood there dreaming at her;
At that point, I felt so skewed.

When our lips touched lightly,
The beat of our hearts grew faint.
In that weakened moment,
I wondered, if she was a saint.

I took the labeled wine,
I tried to sell it again.
All that I could feel
Was weakened knees in Zen.

So, now when I dare see her,
Out of my darkened deepest dreams,
I still wonder if her heart beats
Like mine, or am I even seen?

Though that kiss was far away,
In silent moments bred,
I still feel that symphony

Of her silence in my head.

Her reservations known to me,
Will only keep me company.
In that graceful place of knowing
That she keeps a silent space for me.

Secrets in the Mouth.

"Shhh. Be quiet," she said.
"Up there, on the mountain top!
Is where you were bred."

I am tired of all your fights.
Just hang up your guns tonight.

"Shhh. Be quiet!" she dreamed,
Wondering if things would be
As they seemed.

She whispered, "That little girl,
With the little curl
Will no longer be silent."

They found there,
At the top of the mound,
The secret pedophile.

2 Trickster Sons

"Sure! You can get a ride.
I have nothing here to hide."

"Sure! Jump in.
I have room here.
I will take you.
You need no fear."

Sneaky, snaky, trickster sons
With masks of smiles
And witches' guns.
Secrets whispered,
Along the way.
"Here! A sound.
For your safety, I am afraid.
Let me be the hound."

"Sure! Let's take a minute here.
I see you wish I have no fear."

The trickster sons had a game to play.
They would not a moment delay.
Trickster 1 took the back,
To see what caused the lack.

Trickster 2 took the front,

Around the side with a grunt.

"Around this side in the back,
This is where your ride does lack.
Just a minute. Let me go.
I have a way to fix and know."

While that nice ride did wait,
In the back it was too late.
Trickster 1 and 2 had gone
With that ride into the sun.

The Man with the Black Gloves

The ritual aligned that day.
The man with the black gloves array.

The ladies pilled on towers of legs,
Like a triangle up to slay.

The man with the gloves looked at me;
I could not see what he would display.

Day turned to night. With it came
The ritual of the black gloves to stay.

For the Blue-Eyed/Red-Eyed Boy

There he was, that little boy.
Uncommon it is true.
He looked up to the sky
With big red eyes of blue.

I asked him, "Why?" His eyes were red,
Especially 'cuz they were blue.
That little boy with kindness said,
"Because, I am not you."

I told that little boy,
With eyes both red and blue,

That I too knew eyes of red,
When I was little too.

So, even though, your eyes are blue.
The red it still shines through.
So "please," I asked the little boy,
"Show me eyes of blue."

When the little boy did cry,
His wails were like the sun.
The sun it burned of red,
Until the day was done.

And when that gentle sun did set,
The blue sky it did show,
All the little tiny things,
That blue-eyed boy did know.

I ask that blue-eyed, red-eyed boy,
To tell me what he knows.
When the blue-eyed boy does tell,
The red-eyed sun will show.

Mangled? Our Question.
"Take me! I am yours."
The heat built like fire.
"I will not hurt you,
Though I am sore.

I am torn without you."

"We will birth something new.
Not mangled like me, or our love.
Trust me, we will be birthed anew,
Wild as the righted wrongs."

Trusting led to birth.
Birth led to dying.
The mangled sang their song,
No songs worth crying.

"Oh! But, we are not mangled,
It just burns like the sun.
Think of it as our love
Burning bright as one."

Perspective held her closer.
The mangled truth, it slept.
At least it was worth trying.
Yet, after all, we wept.

The Shroud

There!
It was.

On that ill-gotten morning.

I could have been surprised,
But it was to be expected.

Nothing more but a bloody vision
Of something I thought was forbidden.

There it was!
That ring
I thought so precious.

Bloody and bloodied
With the stains of retribution.

"I was married!" I thought.
"To the death, and blood of it all."

Together, my life,
My ring,
And the shroud.
But, it was bloody.
Surfacing,

In the morning light.

See plainly,
The bleak,
Treacherous death of it all.

I smiled
At the bloody vision
In my mind.

The ring
Even surprised me.
Its wealth,
Its promises.

I tried
To wash it off.

The blood
Still dripped
On that sacred cloth.

No Regard

In the quiet of that dismal place,
My animal failed to regard.

In that state of dreary bliss,
My animal failed to guard.

The wicked dark and dungeon,
Could not make me smile.

I was myself,
But I was not.

In that heaping pile.

The Children at the Bottom

"Give me. Give me.
I have none,"
said the child
To the weeping sun.

"But, I will take.
I will take it back.
No sorrow,
No need for lack."

"Burn me! You will,
A soul yet to fulfill."

I cannot silence
Such a muse.
For in that silence
Is much abuse.

"Take me! Take me!
I am yours.
But you will never
Have me still."

"Awaken! Awaken!
All is gold.
But, pyrite

Is the lack to fill."

"I will not silence,
Give me now.
I will take it again.
That is a vow."

"In all your streams
Of naked dreams.
I will never be
What I seem."

The Rainbow and the Dark Raven

I could see it in his eyes,
That dark longing to remember.

His eyes were mystic,
He would not surrender.

In that fierce abode that was his mind,
He kept his essence sheltered.

He saw the colors of the sun,
With that sun, came the swelter.

He wracked his brain to try to remember,
All the colors that it could tell.
But, the darkness of the Raven
Could not his mind expel?

What if the sun could bring again,
The light into the rainbow?

But that light was fading fast,
The dark Raven was the crescendo.

The Wanting Lack

They were black and cool.

Eyes like mystic eyes,
I had never seen.

My thoughts would have been
Played a fool.

But, he had his garden gleam.

"There!
Underneath this broken bed."

"I will tell you all you want to know."
That bed it bled,
A solemn silence
I could never know.

"A time machine?
Will it take me back?
To that blizzard
Where your mother lacked?"

In the dollar signs and bills,
Was a lack left to be fulfilled?

The empty songs sang,
As I rode on that plane.

In that time machine,
Where I was insane.

To see that mother left alone,
In her illness a secret was known.

Now, in those dark
And beckoning eyes,
I see a dream!

A time machine, that flies.
When I come back home, I see
The lack that was
Fulfilled in me.

The Conversation

"You don't understand…"
she said.
"It's in the impulse.
It's in the idea
Of what you had."

"But, I want control,"
he said.
"It's in the impulse,
And the dream
Of what I want."

"It's negotiable,"
she stated.
"It's the idea
Of my choice,
My life,
My will.
This is what confronts."
"What I want,
I take,"
he stated.
"Without recourse
Without second thought."

She cried,

"You can have it raw.
You can have it rude.
It's my choice,
My body,
My fuel."

She walked away
That day,
From that rude boy
With his way.

She made a point,
In that conversation.

He wasn't wrong.

That truth
Was her elation.

The Strange Situation

She called him
On that day.

She felt her mind
Would go astray.

"Come, my love.
Help me now.
The way from me
To you has passed."

She waited
For his voice.

The voice she felt
So familiar.

The consistent voice.
The voice she knew
As her own.

Another voice answered,
"Hello?"
It said,
"Your love is not here."

It spoke
With solemn fear.

"His sister and his love
Have vanished
Into the world beyond."

"They fled for fear.
The world they burnt down
Is here."

"The Law!
They suspect them both."

"The end could be
The worst."

"Do not fear now.
Your love will come."

"Meet him
In the morning sun."

"But, if he does
Not come,
The light will guide
You on your way."

"Either way,
You will be OK."

The young girl,
Envisioned in her mind,

What could have
Happened to her kind?

She saw the burning
Rubble fall.

In that tale
Betrayal all.

She called to her lover,
"Come to me."

But, in that love
The darkest sea.

She could not dial
Enough times.

To find the strings
So unaligned.

When that

Wounded darkness came,

She felt her voice.

She feigned
She was sane.

She heard the sister
In the quiet.

She felt her thunder
In the darkness riot.

"Where is my lover?
Come to me."

In the deserted darkness
A lover's plea.

"Quiet now, so I can hear."
"I feel him closer
With each breath so near."

The other voice
Came aloud.

"Do not seek him
In this crowd.

For in the darkness,
The rioting womb.

A sister's voice
Will blossom through."

"Lover, lover!
Please come to me."

The weeping kneeled
Lovely plea.

In that softly burning
Flame,

Another sister
Would shame to stain.

The Peculiar Moment

There I was
In that stalled moment.

I felt that peculiar feast
Feeding on my veins.

I looked behind me
To see what it was.

Was it an angel?
Was it a demon?

It was something
So peculiar and obvious.

Something in between
The worlds unseen.

There she smiled at me.

I looked to find him
Standing before me.

I wanted him to ignore.
He was distant.

"There is nothing there,
My love.
Nothing for you to see."

But, there the pleasure
Lingered behind me.

Penetrating me,
In that difficult place.

In the world of
Peculiar experiences.

Atlantis and the Womb

His hands made of iron.
His eyes blackened with stone.

He crept down,
(As monstrous as he was)
Into the great unknown.

He was looking for something clever.
He was digging for sights unseen.
His mind was fixed on that golden empire,
Of gods and goddesses so keen.

He crept into her bed,

With his one open, naked eye.

The other was masked.
It would die.

He rushed with the wind,
Though he had no hair.

He found in her womb,
A secret lair.

A shiny-like gold,
Sparkled in his eye.

He did not blink,
Or even sigh.

The cradles and carriages,
That sat in her womb.

Rested surely,
This was their tomb.
They sat shackled against the rims,
As the cradles rattled in the winds.

The monster smelled each wind that passed,
His longing for gold was in his grasp.

There in the sinking seas of wind,
The womb carried more for him.

There the children would have no rest,
This monster they would fear and detest.

This gruesome thing would devour,
All of the children's sacred power.

The abnormal fiendish, friendless foe,
Crawled in her womb, he was woe.

He heard their fearful sounds,
His obscenity upon their grounds.

They tried to mask their energy,
With fearless hope, and longing memory.

The grotesque beast smelled their fright,
He turned around to meet their fight.
He could smell their leaking silent sounds,
He was a gruesome, terrible hound.

The princess in a land far, far away,
Sat softly with her lord array.

Her beautiful hair, long and red,
Christened her shoulders, naked and bare.

The lord was certain that all would stare,
His love and riches he would bear.

Leave riches a'far?
He would not care.

For the love of her,
The soldiers came,
All dressed in black.

Their masks of greed,
Held certain lack.

They crept up into his lair,
They winded and wriggled
Up his stairs.

They searched for more
Than he could give.
"Upwards! Forwards!
Swords, and spears."

The lord with his lady came.
They were christened,
By masks of shame.

"Do you not care, for riches fair?
We think this ought not

Be your lair."

"Underneath your lady's gown,
We see your weakened,
Awful crown."

"Do not mind if we seize and steal.
Mind us not, if we take your will."

"We will war for riches found.
We will take your precious crown."

Soon, the monstrous one in her,
Rose to the surface and found his world.

Now that wars and battles were fought,
All would come to a disastrous lot.

The children would find no more womb,
For that womb would be their tomb.

When the war came alive,
All the precious beauty died.

The naked ladies bore their swords,
The sand, the ceiling was a horror.

They crawled and fought.

They looted and begged.

All they had,
Was more dread.

In that weakened hour of change,
That wounded womb her soul exchanged.

Then she howled to the moon.
Her children in her, their own precious tomb.

She would no longer wink and wait.
She would no longer take their bait.
In the rising, burning sun,
Where the sand did beat its drum.

She took her womb strands in her hands.
She built a wall to crush their lands.

So, in the womb that now was doomed.
She found for them a sacred tomb.

Rush and crush and rise so high!
This wall of womb in their naked eye.

The fiendish eye of the monster dread,
Would find her womb fall over his head.

Now the wall of womb did rise,
And all the gods were left to hide.
In the rising falling sand,
Under the great womb command.

The goddesses cried for their suns!
The womb, her web was then spun.

The winding winds then took their vow,
To take the womb and wipe them out.

The Buddha and the Pupil

The Buddha says,
"You want to travel to where the stars begin?"

The pupil says,
"Yes! But, where do the stars begin?"

The Buddha says,
"That is not the question."

The pupil says,
"I want to travel to where the stars end."

The Buddha says,
"Where do the stars end?"

The pupil says,
"Yes! Where do the stars end?"

The Buddha says,
"That is not the question."

The pupil says,
"What is the question?"

The Buddha says,
"Where do you end?"

The pupil says,
"Where the stars end."

The Buddha says,
"Then, what is the question?"

The pupil says,
"Where do I end?"

The Buddha says,
"Yes! Now you understand more.
But, what is the question?"

The pupil says,
"Where do I begin?"

The Buddha says,
"Yes! But where do you end?"

The pupil says,
"Yes! I understand."

"I begin where the stars begin.
I end where the stars end."

The Buddha says,
"Closer. But, do the stars ever end?"

The pupil says,
"I don't know. Do they?"

The Buddha says,
"What is the answer?"

The pupil says,
"Yes. I see. I understand now."

"The stars never end.
The stars only begin."

The Buddha says,
"Yes. Then, what is the question?"

The pupil says,
"Do I end?
Or, do I only begin?"

The Buddha says,
"Yes. Well, what is the answer?"
The pupil says,
"I am the stars.
I begin.
I never end."

The Buddha smiled and said,
"So, you want to travel

To where the stars begin?"

The pupil says,
"I am already here.
I am where the stars begin."

The Buddha says no more.

Who Killed the Elephant?

There was this glorious elephant,
He was all decked in gold.

He had rubies between his eyes,
His story was loud and bold.

On his back was a royal robe,
His trunk lifted high toward the sky.
His sound was loud and heavy,
Of its power, no one would question why.

One day that elephant met his doom,
When he sang his song into the sky.

His innocence eclipsed each song,
This elephant was gracious, he would cry.

He presumed all hosts to be gracious,
He opened his doors to all that came.

One wicked ruler came one wicked night,
He stabbed the elephant just the same.

He took his ruler and cut him hard.
He stuck the elephant like a pig.

He scarred that elephant with his rule.
As the elephant died, the ruler danced a jig.

The golden and purple royal robes,
Fell to the ground, along with its crown.

The elephant stood perplexed and sad,
Until the elephant fell to the ground.
The people who loved this elephant so,
Cried out to the killer ruler, "Stop this cruelty!"

The ruler ignored the people, watched the blood,
Denying the elephant a sense of divinity.

After the ruler pulled out his rule,
The elephant bled until he could bleed no more.

The ruler smiled in his deadly success.
He left the dying elephant on the floor.

The people came to the dying elephant,
They cried and wept for their love.

They took the robes of gold and purple,
They took the ruby and placed it high above.

The sky looked dark; the sky it rained.
All the people held hands and danced.

They danced around, and around, and around.
They would not let him die; they took a stance.

They waited nights, they waited days,
For the elephant to come alive again.
One day the people closed their eyes.
They kept their song, they would not refrain.

As they slept still singing their song,
They went off to dream of their elephant strong.

The morning came, they opened their eyes.
Only the robes and rubies were left, this was wrong.

The elephant had suddenly disappeared,
They could not see where the body had gone.

They cried out, "Help us find where the elephant went!"
They cried all day until the night came.

They closed their eyes as their lids grew faint,
They were weary from the tears that drained.

They all laid down, one body resting on the other.
They waited for dreams to cease their pain.

In their dreams, they all remembered.
What each of them saw, was just the same.

The gracious elephant was lifted high!
He stood with his gold, ruby, and robes.

His eyes were bright; his song was alive.
He sang and he sang as the story goes.

The elephant's radiant song, it burst,
All through the galaxies in the Universe.

He shone like the sun; he would never die.
Even though the ruler murdered him first.

The Secret Boys

"Why do you look at me?"

My eyes blink.

"I am flirtatious.
Can you see me?"

"Why do come toward me?"

Like a silent boy
That wanders?

"What makes you see me?"
"I saw you coming."

"You came to me,
Eyes flashing,
Flirting and squinting
With the sun."

You see me so innocent.

"Who do you think
I AM?"

Was it my eyes that

Gave me away?

"What if I tell you
The innocence in my eyes
Is only a reflection
Of something you
Do not know?"

It is a revelation
Of something.

I cannot tell.

"Come to me, regardless.
I cannot care."

"But you will care.
My eyes that shine
Are dimmed
By your embrace."

I am the secret.

I am the lover
Of your father.

"Shine on me."

"Let me see
My own lies."

Come to me.

"I am disappointment."

"I will scar you
For life."

"I will make you
Walk on a bed
Of snakes."

"I will see our mother
Drown you
In our embrace."

Cradle me now.

"I knew
I could not
Hide from you."

"I will hide
My gentle eyes
In the storm."

"Of my oblivion,
Created by your jealousy."

"Real as the wounds
In my heart."

See my flirtatious eyes?

Trembling at your
Existence.

"Come to me
As a pile of snakes."

"Come to me in waves
Of the ocean."

"I will burry my past
In my tears."

In your awakening.

In your revenge.

"I will master my fears."

The Burning

She was new in town.

Her body was old,
Her mind was quick.

She left her mark
On the rings of fire
That crept encrypted.

She sang her song
Into the vision on the screen.

She smiled a wicked smile.

She was to challenge them,
All the feeble-minded frowns.
She would make them laugh.

She would be the unseen.

She was the spirit
Of their sardonic dreams.

There was her day to rise.

She sang her song

Aloud.

She smiled into the summer.

There he was,
That one.
That perfect flower.
That mask of energy basking.

He basked in all that was sexy.

He dreamed in all that was cool.

He would be the player.

She struck him underneath.

In that place,
Where life
Burns
And turns,
Crazy like stains.

She supplicated to him a favor.
She would take him down,
To that place where humor burns.

That morning the world awakened.

It watched from that gleaming.

But, there was a burning sight to be seen.
There that comedic lady,
In all her old and witchy ways,
Was young again.
Like her jeans.

"Laugh a while.
Play for a time,"
she said.

With a spark relayed,
To the innocence and wonder.

She spoke again,
With thunder.

"Come, my prince.
Show me!
Give me your naked ways."

Her body shifted like a snake.

Her age was gone,
Disappearing in her muscles.

They bulged and protruded.

Her arms built her body around.
The jeans she wore,
Covered her sacred ground.

Never a sacred space in that burn.

"Take me," he said.

That naked dream.

"Oh, baby.
That is the only way."

She took him like a clown.

The burn would shine,
On the seeds that would dream.

Of a naked man, and a burn.

If We Let You In

Dance with us
Just a bit more.

We long to surf
And swim ashore.

The long streets,
They call our name.

We walk and walk
Just the same.

You pretty boys
In your silken suits.

You lovely girls
In your quiet muse.

You dance for us
Around the corner shores.

You dream a dream,
And fantasy ignores.

Tell us of your voices quaint,
We will observe your name.

Can you be a bit less discrete?
Quiet the mind,
Be complete.
Your pretty faces
And your funny books.

Where's the party,
Where are the other looks?

Here, come in!
We have nothing to hide.

In our books,
Your party will thrive.

Chase me down?
How could you now?

Your books,
Your books,
In and out.

But, the storm, it comes,
Without a doubt.

The dancing girl
Just sat with a pout.

Go on and claim
The death of us all.

Eat your books,
Drown and crawl.

But I know,
Dancing,
Wild and free.

Your books,
One day,
Will crawl to me.

The Cat and the Snake

Wrestle with me!

Scratch...
Tear...
Drown.

I will see
No more
Of this!

Take my claws.
Scratch...
Scrape away.

Dig deep,
With talons
Long and fierce.

My head
Will be wounded,
For now.

But in death,
I will retake.

The head

Lay bruised,
Buried still.

That head
Of fire

That head
Of will

Crushed,
It fell,
With no
More time.

The stricken
Was struck.

The claws
Were the strife.

The head,
It fell,
Under those talons.

The soul
Of the talons
Fell into
Madness.

Crushed...
Lay the head.

Its value,
Laid waste.

All of this,
The crusher's taste.

The Obnoxious Lady, and the One Who Tried

Her belly was full of laughter.
It rolled arrogantly in the wind.

"Ha! Ha! Ha!"
She laughed.

The One smiled,
Eager to please her.

"Here! This is for you...
And this, and that,
And that, and this.
These are my gifts.
They are all for you!

The obnoxious lady,
She took and took.

She was greedy
For the pleasure of it all.

"Yes! Give me more.
Yes! I want it all.
Give me! Give me!
Give me!"

The house was filled
With laughter.

The One was eager to please.

Her children came in running.
Their feet clapped like thunder.
Their bodies crashed like lightning.

The obnoxious lady turned
To see what the One was doing.

"Out! Get out!" she said.
"My children are here,
I need you no longer."

"But this was all for you!
These gifts that I brought you.
Here! I have more.
Take! Take! Take!"

The children snickered.

"That one is a fool.
He stole those gifts from another.
Those gifts are not the One's to give."

The obnoxious lady scowled
And growled,
"See! You are a liar and a thief.
Out! Before I betray you further."

The One, with his head down
And his eyes sulked,
Turned.
In desperation,
The One tried
To pick up what was left of his gifts.

But, there was only bits and pieces left.
In his sadness,
He wondered,
Were his gifts stolen all along?

The Dark Ego

There was nothing of more pure evil.

One intention.

One motive.

Take to take, and to devour.

The servant could only serve the dark ego,
And stay out of its way.

The dark ego,
The pure monster.

Gives nothing.

Will share nothing.

The servant will serve,
And stay out of its way.

Or the dark ego
Will take the servant as prey.

The Exposed

He was perfect
In all of his light.

He was majestic
In his own delight.

She stood beneath.
She looked above.

She tore off the wig.
There was nothing
But love.

But, underneath
That guise of truth,

Was the hair that grew
To speak its truth.

The days went solemn.
The eyes grew numb.

The was nothing new
Under the sun.

For when that wig,
It was torn off.

The hair that grew
Was silent and soft.

There was nothing more
A man could say.

The wig and the hair
Was all an array.

So, when she shed,
The layers fell.

And what was left
Were secrets to tell.

"So don't you think
Of tearing it off?"

"Unless your will
Is as strong as your loft."

For all the songs
Left to be told,

You would find the vacant
And the bold.

"So tear your own wig.
Tear it off."

"For underneath,
You will find what's not."

Even though
You shed and shed,

The wig will always
Tear in red.

"Tear it! Crumble it!
Make it bold!"

Underneath,
The mind will unfold.

So, blond or black
Or brown or red,

There will always be
More of mind to shed.

Fill Me! ...What Was Empty?

So many things...

"So beautiful!"
she said.

"I can have this
Or that!
I like the hat,
As long as
It doesn't make
Me fat."

The lady laughed.

"Oh, yes!"

She said evened in pace,

"I like the hat."

For better
Or for worse,
The hat christens you;
It is not a curse.

In your reflection,
In your guise,
I see your beautiful,

Open eyes.
So, wear that hat,
And talk to your soul.
You are a beauty,
I see your soul.

The Different One: His Song

He looked at me.

He was an It.

His rhythms fell and fell down.

He was not a clown,
But his mind was wit.

He would not keep it down.
He took his arms,
He raged and roared.

They moved
In contortions
I once had ignored.

But even with his mask
So loud,
I saw him in
A twitching cloud.

Not Mine.

Her mind:
Deliberated.

His mind:
Aloof.

He appeared.
He was a mist.

She saw him.
She only felt.
He came in
With a child

At his breast,
His wild.

"I want you
To be mine,"

She said,
Like a chime.

"I am here.
Why the question?"

She quivered.

"The child,
It is not yours,"
he said knowingly,

A wink in his eye.

"I know,"
she said.

I understood
Before.

"I want
To be with you."

She poured out
Her heart and soul.

"I am here,"
he said,
Unwaveringly.

She smiled
At the child.

She said,
"I already know."

Words spoken,
Reminded her.
"I am here.
Already here."

The Projection

The lines were blurred,
The streams were mangled,
The craft was broken,
Yet it was fulfilled.

The signs gone out
Were stricken.
The lights blurred black
And red.

The people shuttered,
Their windows broken.
Their songs were dead.

They climbed forward,
Just to see nothing.
The windows,
With their chimes that bled.

They broke open,
Nothing blessed.
They still spoke,
With wings for words.

The echoes scrambled
Backward and forward.

They climbed into minds,
Their hearts were blurred.

In their hearts,
The words were spoken.
A curse to their memories
Of vacant times.

She sat there waiting,
Her power growing.
She couldn't believe
That success was hers.

She found the demon,
Large and lurking,
To disrupt
Her choice of words.

Where am I?
She spoke into the nothing.
What did you steal?
Or, what do you gain?

Wake me, I want to not be broken.
I sent the sounds that broke them.
Is that now, my disdain?
Or, what drove me insane?

Wake me now!
What have you done?
Her delirium growing,
With the setting sun.

Here!
Take it back.
We want nothing more
Of you.

We saw you sitting,
Mind a token.
When we found you,
You were undone.

So take back what you stole;
Your mind will be,
In this looping hole
Of our fantasy.

You will find the air
Is fresh and empty.
A sword in your mind
Will your flesh grow?

So the winded worlds
Of soft and plenty,
To take for taste

And then for some.

Will bleed the emptiness
In what is broken.
Her mind laid
With the setting sun.

The Space Changers

Oblivion brought unseen hope.
In masks of time, they came and went.
The fires that blazed in the night
Were torches. Burnt us to our death.
Time itself would not allow it.
The changers came, and in time they left.
The winds did not blow, the signs did not show;
But, the changers came and went.
All the fires raging below took the flame;
They took it with their bow.
Their metal boundaries kept them fixed
On the target in their timeline mix.
In and out, they came and then were gone;
No need for wind, no need for sun.
In the blackness, their time it slept;
Until the changers came and went.

The Corroded Fire and the Dancing Girl

There she burned in the concrete desert.
No mind to bare or be her own.

There he stared like an ugly peasant,
To grasp and grovel; her he could know.

The broken concrete fell rotting.
The damsel on fire danced and spun.

The fire blazed with words unspoken.
She danced into the setting sun.

The Fish-God with Hazel Eyes

Oh womb! Birth! She cried.
Her hair fell down her shoulders,
Crowding her body with delight.

Oh, yes! A son! He cried.
His eyes like the moon shining.
It was beaming bright, barely night.

There the little spawn,
Wiggled its way to the sand.
It creeped away and out of sight.

Oh! Where is our son?
They gasped with breathlessness.
Had they lost him to the night?

Oh! Dig and Dig! We must dig!
We lost him into the creeping sand.
We cannot lose him. Oh! The fright!

Suddenly! Up and between their feet,
Intertwining around their legs,
The Fish-god exploded with might!

His eyes were brown and green,
His body lean. His tail whipped round.

He was the song and charm of their light!

Oh! His eyes are rare and beyond compare!
He turns like a fish with his tail around!
We will love him without shame or spite.

The fish-tailed god spun around.
He wrapped around the bordering sand.
He would be the fish-god of eternal delight!

No other fish-god could compare!
He could reach to the sea and to the sky.
He disappeared into the sand with a sigh!

The Fearless One
(Dedicated to my brother, Michael)

She hadn't seen him for many moons,
But, there he appeared in a good mood.

"What was it," she asked, "that pulled you away?"
"It was five or so years since I have seen you this way."

He winked with a smirk. "Hey, I am no jerk!"

"It could have been five. It could have been ten."
"What's up with your quirk? Trying to label me then?"

She said, "Hey, that's okay. Good to know your way."
"Glad that didn't happen. But, I want you to stay."

He smiled a bit, then disappeared to the sky.
I thought he was carrying me way up high.

I saw the veins of the city below.
I wondered if it were, just the undertow.
(But, you never know!)

One sees a demon. One sees an angel. Their opinions to
bestow.

"I am frightened. Grip me tight. This flight is out of
sight!"
"Don't loosen your grip. My fear catches me down in it."

He said, "Oh! Don't be foolish, you squirmy girl."
"I know your one little curl. And, your fear to whirl."

"I could drop you down, but you wouldn't die."
"For death itself, you would deny."

"Oh, don't you feel the rapture? Way up high?"
"Can't you feel the freedom in my eye?"

She flew so sullen, under his grip.
With a map of the Universe, he was equipped.

Her stomach floated with each and every breeze.
To know him was to love him, with such amazing ease.

He had her in his grip. Tease? Oh, please!

The Wind

She crashed into me.
I was devoured by her.

She tore me around.

She brought me
Up and down many shores.

She caught me
In a drift of time.

I did not know her,
But she was mine.

She pulled my hair;
She drowned my soul.

She took my house,
She left me bare.

I was naked,
Standing there.

The roofs were taken.
My arms were torn.

She twirled and whirled
Around the night.

She took my eyes,
Barren of light.

I wanted to strike
Her down
With all my might.

I cursed at her soul.
I angered at her sight.

Then, so strange--
She spoke to me.

"I am mightier
Than light."

She said,
"I am here.
I am gone."

She said,
"I am wind.
I am might."

"So all your curses,

They will fail.

But, my light
Will stand tonight."

"So, if you choose
To fight,

I will keep you
Up all night."

"Your children,
Your wombs,

Will feel
The wrath
Of my tombs."

She shielded her eyes.
Her voice crept into my soul.

She said,
"So kiss me now,
Before I go."

"I will come again,
This you must know."

"Kindle me a fire.
Light it bright.

I will come
For you tonight."

There I stood,
In the wind.

I felt her curses,
I felt my stains.

I took her in,
Yet I remained.

With my barren arms,
I embraced her soul.

All night long--
Forevermore.

She touched my cheeks.
She lit her fire.

The houses were gone,
But not my empire.

With the leaves,

She laid naked there—

I found her perfect,
Powerful stare.

In that vacant
Flare of nothing,

I began to see her--
She was something.

I was left naked,
At her touch.

The gentle wind,
Comforted me much.

I will always
Honor her now.

That will be
My sacred vow.

So when she
Will come again,

I will always
Embrace the wind.

Here beneath
This empire of dust,
I will the wind
Choose to trust.

So chant with me
This sacred vow,

And with these words
You will find somehow,

A way to feel
The master she is,

And with her power
She will reveal.

The Wind Chant

"I embrace the wind,
The wind embraces me.

You embrace the wind,
The wind embraces you.

We embrace the wind,
The wind embraces us."

The Moon

Moon, moon, hanging there!
How is
Your
Garden fair?

Hanging beneath
The weeping willows,
With the stars
Oh so fair?

Moon, moon, hanging there!
How do your
Willows cry?

Up with
The stars
So high?

Moon, moon, with your light
So rare.
Do you see us,
Underneath your stare?

Moon, moon, in all your glory!
Do you see our light?
Know our stories?

Moon, moon, weeping moon!
Will you come
Again soon?

Moon, moon, love of mine!
I will stay
With you and shine.

Moon, moon, for all I see!
Is your light
Shining back at me?

The Waterfalls

Where do the waterfalls go?

Down to the deepest shore—

Where the fish can swim no more.

To the shallow water shore—

Forevermore.

The Matador and the Bull: a Story.
How that bull gave the matador a run for his money.

There was the matador,
Strong in his breath and strength;
He was ready for the bull,
He cared not if she would blink.

He made his peace with the demons in his mind;
He knew the bull would be his "mine."
He strode along the dirty floor,
He sang his song of matador.

There he waited with bated breath.
He hoped to see its death.

There the gates did open for
That hungry, greedy matador.

And just outside that luminous gate,
The matador, he did wait.
And oh that bull that had him fill,
Was onward over just to kill.

The bull rode onward, forward.
He bucked and pulled that matador.
The matador in his foolish wit
Thought the red flag up for it.
When that matador did ride,

He saw his own suicide.
That crazy bull just would not quit.
The matador was not fit.

So the matador did ride,
That crazy matador met suicide.
The bull danced 'round, flaunting his pride,
That matador, yes, he died.

The Shy One—Dedicated to Mathew Shephard

"Oh! No," he said.
"She likes you. It's a date!"

I hope she does not come too late.

Oh, you strange, peculiar thing.

I saw you smiling.

Oh! Without a doubt, she comes
With the setting, sinking suns.

"She comes to you,
All wild and free."
But you—you have your eyes for me.

"Sucks to you, you pagan whore."

You know you always wanted more.

"But it's a secure, sure thing.
I might even buy her a ring."

You liar, look me in my eyes.
Tell me you can see your lies.

He turned around and walked away;
He would tell his story another day.

That day he bought her flowers and all.
He even bought her a pretty shawl.

She arrived a tad too late.

It's true.
He was all nerves and brew.

His heart, he tried to make it wait.

He wanted to see her and anticipate.

The gleeful cherry tree look in her eyes.
The apples that glittered between her thighs.

He stood with a corny look on his face,
Hoping he wouldn't her glamour disgrace.

When there in the shadows,
Her reflection came.

He might as well have thought
Himself insane.

Her very eyes blemished their every move.
Her hips were large,

Her stench was crude.

He tried to cuddle up to her smile.
But, he feared he would his own face defile.
He gave her flowers and bowed to her well.
But then he ran like a bat out of hell.

There, in the corridors of the concrete halls,
The shy one crept, knowing his falls.

The shy one looked on, oh so well.
His shadows would be his redemption from hell.

"Oh! It's you, I see. I run aghast.
That vile woman would have me at last."

But, oh! Make me run for once and all.
My shy one will bless my fall.

The Eyes

Strange to walk
With eyes that stare
At my back
Through the window,
Creeping up against
My shadow that falls behind,
Fearless, regardless.
His eyes only a trap
To hide the truth.
Pin me down
To the ground.
One shoulder held,
The other one pinned.
His eyes shifted.
Now, I can see
They are black widows,
Turning back in,
Rolling again.
I am immune.
So the eyes walk
Away into the night,
Sitting by the window,
Again, following
My shadow.

Where There is Nothing

It was a quaint moment of silence
Where he betrayed his emotions.

Running away...fumbling.

He saw her, but she wasn't really there.
All in his imagination, he envisioned her stare.

Staying alive and awake within him.

He toyed with wondering where she could be.
He played with the science of everything, endearing.

Staying far away.

Far away from reality, he saw her.
She was a ghost in his mind, a dream.

She eluded him, running away.

He closed his eyes, though the moon shone bright,
He shut his mind off like a switch...there, then gone.
Feeling her, wanting her to stay.

When he opened his eyes again,
He could not, but recognize the state he was in.

There he smelt her, like life, like poison.

He was enraptured, so sudden in his dreary state,
He dared not want this dream to be over.

To create, to create, what would he create?

Over and over he suffocated, dying for her voice.
But she screamed so loud her confusion,

That he was lying, dreaming, dying.

When he closed his eyes, he could see her.
She did this to him, but it was all his fault.

He invented her; she was there because of him.

He wanted to cry, for her to leave him be,
But he wanted her as much as he desired to leave.

She beckoned him, to stay...stay...stay.

He longed to feel that something didn't separate them,
But a dream was only an escape, from what?

Reality, reality pulled him hard, pulled him away.

Her heart, he fathomed, would feel his own.

Her feelings, he fathomed, would trace his own.

Wanting, longing, time passing.
For a second he paused, he longed.
He wanted to hear the whisper of his pillow.

Of the sacred vault that would carry him home.

Far away from her, her ghost, haunting, dead.
Where do whispers stop? he asked himself.

If only he had a code to stop the aching silence.
If only he could be a dream.

He heard her, but the veils of silence called him.
Run...reap...run...sleep...go home.

Where was home? Running, staying, falling?

Should he leave his eyes open, should he shut them
Tight as the swollen tears in his eyes?

She could return. She would come back.

The silence was broken with a single stare,
His own reflection haunted him like a secret stain.

He waited. Waited longer. Waiting.

Then, he felt her. Her serpent intertwined his own.
It crawled and reaped the harvest of his belly.

Bloated...empty...on fire...swollen with sorrow.

He could never leave, he knew, though he pulled,
Hard against the earth and the swollen belly.

Filled, empty, swollen, empty but only hers.

She longed to fill it, but it crumbled in her grasp.
He would have seen, but blinded eyes can do nothing.

Grasping, reaching, crawling, crying, knowing nothing.

Where was there any choice? Where was there leaving
Or coming? Or staying? Or going? When was there...

Anything? Disappearing into the lack, the void.

Coming again, she stood. Head held high, heart in
bandages,
Brocaded by her own heart. Open but closed.

Will the will never end? Never die?

Take me in, set me free. Let me loose. Devour me.
Cry. Take. Love. Kill. Die. You are only dreaming.

Conquer me. Conquering.

He did not need to take her with him. She was she.
She was already there. She was already gone.

Vapor. Violent storm. Thunderous awakening.

Beckoning death among the creases of life.
Calling home in the vacant spots of pain.

Longing. Revealing. Calling.

Intertwined...completely whole, amongst them
The songs of empty winds, in the voices of nothing.

Reaping. Sowing...tumultuous...long.

The Girl with the Pyramid

"Silence," she said.
Eyes wide open.

"They will not know
The difference."

She whispered,
"Gratitude is a soft sound,
A whisperer of secrets."

"What are your secrets?"
she asked them. "Pray tell."

Running away, into the arms.
Egypt calls...whispers run.
Nothing is new
Under the sun.

Trace back the numbers,
But there were none
To be found.

She stood on the silence
Of broken and sacred
Ground.

"I hold it here,
Your pyramid."

Which way did she go?
No one would ever know.

Silence and gratitude
Reaped the pyramid she sowed.

Frightened

"It will be easier this way."

She thought nothing of it,
Trying on his big, green pants.

"It's okay," she told herself.
"I mean, I am only trying to understand."

The pants fit, big and baggy.
The green was army green:
Solid, with shades of gray.

There he was, in her heart.
She could not bear
To walk away.

"I think I will stay," she said.
"Wearing these big, green pants."

The phone rang.

She answered, "Hello?"
"Hello?"

He asked her
What she meant by

Her wearing his
Big, baggy, green pants.

She said, "I am trying
To understand."

He said, "What?"

She said, "Why
I am so frightened."
Should I be?"

"Maybe," he said.

She said, "Maybe I should."
Dumbfounded.

Broken Confidence

He was always there...

Too much.
Too easy.
Too loyal.
Too soon.

"I will run away,"
she said.
"Run away from you!"

She pondered.

Better things?
Other things?
Other muses?
Other strings?

No lack could find
Her there.

All was left behind,
Including his stare.

Travel on.

She will!

She might!
Oh! Fight.
Fight.

Walking away,
Grew harder still.
Her illusions
Shattered, killed.

Run for it!
Run back!
Grasp it!
Don't turn back!

"But, I cannot."
—Run forever more.

I am missing
What I left for sure.

See it!
Chase it!
Disappoint it!
Run!

She sat,
Her heart melting
Into the sinking sun.

It crept.

Where is he?
Where did he go?
Find him?
Panic?
Come back
For more!

She sees him there.
"Run to get him,"
she says.

The door is closed.
He proposed.
Darkness comes over.
Her heart to the floor.

Come back!
No slack!
I have you tracked!
I have cracked!

It was over then,
Her running
From him.

Now he was gone.
Down to his bliss.

The remorseful one...

She cried,
The weeping child,
In the mist.

The Child

Push for me, child of mine.
Push the baby down the road.
Push it gently. Push it slow.
Crowd yourself with your duties.
Run yourself over with giving.
We will take what you can give.
It's your duty to please us.
Can't you see you are nothing?
We will take what we want
From you. We will take your stars.
We will take your moon.
We will take your life and give it to another.
Push the stroller.
Take the new creature into your care.
No matter about the older one
Rubbing against your back like a lion.
The ones you have in your heart.
Push. Push. Push. Push. Push.
We will run you over.
We will take your life.
We will rub against you, working against your will.
Silence child. Push the stroller harder.
We will own you yet.

Survival

Think with me.
I will throw you in the water.
You are dirty.
Your family is rotten.
But, you will learn quickly
What it means to survive.

Splash!!! Splash!!! Splash!!!

The water curved around.
Their bodies sank under the water.

The boy the same.
The girl the same.
The mother the same.
The father the same.
No one to blame.

Into the water you go.

The swirls curled around them.
They could have drowned,
But they didn't.
They curved around with the water.
They drank it all into their skin.
They absorbed the death.
They cradled the life

127

Of the water all around them.

Finally! The shore came.
It was easy to understand.
Even though they were famished
And thirsty.
For the ocean, it could not quench
The thirst they felt.
The shore was easy to sink into.
It was easy to find.
To find themselves once again
In the sand.

The boy smelled the fire burning.
The water
Had not destroyed him yet.

Eat it.

Whatever it is,
It couldn't be worse than that.
The water that came,
Tortured and curved around again.

The young boy opened his mouth.
Oh! The flavor would taste so good.
He opened his mouth to taste it,
Safety so sweet.

The water was gone.
The shore had come.
But,
As the boy opened his mouth
To consume the feast,
He opened his eyes to see
It was just a stick.
He was still in the water,
Drinking in his life,
Like the rivers of water
That only seem like life
But taste
As the short end of a stick.

Believe harder.

The young girl said,

Mother and father are here!
The stick is only your imagination,
Killing you like the water,
The very water you drown in.
Believe harder.

The young boy breathed harder
Until the image of the stick
Was gone,
And all that was left
Was the water.

The Privileged Ones

"It's just a school,"
she said.

He wasn't convinced.

"I know it is,"
he said with a wince.

He tried to convince her
But the teacher
Came.

He worried
He would
Struggle in vain.

But, in the end
The sister knew.

"She is just as much
For me as she is for you."
Run, now.
Run away.
The teacher is coming.
Her eyes will say,
And tell us all
What we will be today.

The Vile Boy

It took him seconds to find the knife,
Plunge it deep down inside,
Let the blood flow all around.

Kill it with truth, and with flawless raw ambition.
Fathers and umbilical cords don't hold me down.
Now is the time for a reckoning of truth,
Found in the dismal sounds.
The bombing is coming, but you will miss it all.
Your fear will come when you see the anger,
When you will feel my rage.

Voices Carried Away in the Abyss

Don't follow me.
You don't want me.

In that dirty hole in the ground.
In that awful place that made no sound.

Just leave me alone.
You don't love me.
Leave. Go. Let me go.
Leave me alone.

In that sour abyss.
In that dark, deep, and dirty alley.
In the crevasses of what is now.
For there can never be a tomorrow.

But, I love you,
she said.

I want to feel my body wrapped around yours.
There is no excuse or reason why.
I just chose to love you, and so I do.

Run now. Run away.

Deep in the solemn, sunken sheets.

In the room of despair.
In the place where I like to hide.
Where nothing is there.

Leave me be.
You can't love me.
You can't need me.
Let me disappear.
My karma is coming.
You won't want to see me there.

But, I am already here.
I will not run away.

Then, the twilight disappeared.
The moon rose and the song
Of her heart left him anxious,
Running away.

There came the electrical fire,
The hand and voice of the gods.
They shouted with a unison voice,

Do you believe?

While the twilight disappeared
Into the darkness of the abyss,
The voice she carried

For her love of him
Crackled into the darkness
Until the light came
And once again
Carried her home.

What an explosion of light.

She said,
Where is now?

The voice inside him said,
Dead. But, not dead.

The Arrow

Creeping in the shadows,
No moon,
Only sun.

Running to hide around the corner,
No sight,
No pun.

Around the corner in the sun,
Arrows drawn,
Strike one.

Escape is not an option,
Running
From the one.

Broken

There goes another.

Break,
Break,
Cracked,
Scared.

There goes another.

Humiliated,
Shamed,
Owned,
Despised.

There he was.
Like cruelty,
Lightning,
Thunder,
In my eyes.

Could I run away?

Scared,
Scarred,
Broken.

There she came.

His companion,
His evil twin,
His muse.

There I begged,

Pleading,
Help me.
Refuse.

There she tried,

Wondering,
Wandering,
What?

There I tried

To run,
To escape,
To fly away,
To hide.

There goes another.

Break,
Cracked,
Broken,
Scared.

There he came again.

Cruelty,
Crawling,
Crippled,
Bare.

There she was.

Rescue,
Believe,
Run
Far.

There she cowered.

Break,
Scar,
Shame,
Charge.

There I cried,

No more!
Die!
Blemish!
Disdain!

Finally, at last,

She came.
She came.

Let's run.

I see you,
Run away.
Run far
Away

There we ran,

Through the water,
Under the dam,
In the night.

There he came,

Chasing
Our souls,
To betray
The fire.
There we ran,

Under the water,
Raging,
Insane,
Expire.
There he came,

Coming
For us,
Running
Far.

Then we pushed

Harder,
With anger,
Revenge,
And heart.

Our broken limbs

Bleeding,
Knees
Crawling,
Alive.
There she said,

I am done.
Leave you
Alone.
Goodbye.

There I cried,

Broken,
Sealed

In stone.
Not again.

There I ran,

Faster,
Furious,
Delight
Within.

My anger

Would save
My broken soul
Tonight.

I would ache,
The final
Toll
My might,
My light.

The Grunge Boy

Wandering.

Where to?

Nowhere.

Where from?

Nowhere.

Come closer.

Let me take
A look
At you.

Come closer.

Let me
Smell
The wretch.

The way
You are,

From always

Into now.

You smell

Of porridge,
Of dark musk,
Of rust.

You smell

Of rats,
Of squalor,
Of death.

It's okay!

You can
Come in.

Shower,
Be.

Privacy,

You will
Have it,
Here, now.

Shower,
Be.

The water
Flooded
The mind.

Brown hair
Black with tar
And empty
Strokes.

Complicated,
Far away,
Closer still.

Thank you
For privacy.
It doesn't
Matter much.

I love you,
Grunge boy.

A Quickie

She could not resist.
Wanting him was too fun!

It was easy to devour him,
To let him devour her.

Once?
Twice?
More!
More!
More!

Too much giggling in pleasure.
Too much fun to resist.

The pleasure of him rested in the moment,
But the delight in herself lasted forever.

Once?
Twice?
More!
More!
More!

So what if you're a friend?
She knew she would forever last

In the lusty ways she felt for him.

Once?
Twice?
More!
More!
More!

Again!
Again!
Again!

The White Wedding and the Dark Night

There she was, all dressed in white.
Her velvety smile caressed my eyes.
She was silky smooth.
"Can I kiss you now that the deed is done?"
I asked.
"Of course, I am yours,"
she said, so nurturing and supple.
No more wondering or wandering,
In and out of thought. Curious, teased.
Now she is mine, and I have the key.
Wait!
There is someone at the door.
Should I bother to check who it might be?
Or should I leave them to their misery
And curiosity. Nothing should interrupt us.
This is our pleasure. May they all
Be jealous of our delights.
Oh well! Whoever it is keeps knocking.
They seem to get louder by the minute.
"Hello? Who are you? What do you need?"
I said, rudely interrupted.
"Can't you see we are busy and in love?"
I cracked open the door and there they stood,
All dressed in white, like they were a part of us.
Their faces and hands were black and dark,
Like the night of terror and forebode.

147

Sneaky little snaky thieves.
I knew what they were after.
They wanted my key. THE key.
They wanted to steal away my joy
And plunge it to the bottom of the river,
Dead and bleak like their darkness.
"Where is the key, my love?"
I asked.
I fumbled around for it, but it was missing.
I still had the chain that the key hung from,
But the key was gone.
I could not find it.
"Don't worry, beloved,"
she whispered.
"The key that belongs to us can never
Be lost or stolen. No matter how dark
The night, or black the faces become,
Our love will never die, and the key
To our truth will disappear from our eyes,
Only to reappear in our hearts."
I sank onto the bed as the black night
Approached to bring us into slumber.
I fought hard to keep my faith in our love
Without the key that represented it.
But, my resentment toward the dark thieves
Remained while my love burned hard
Like a sun in the middle of a dark night.

The Tsunami

"Here it comes," I said.
The waves.
"Move forward," he said.
Press on.
"But I like them," I said.
Unafraid.
"Press forward," he said.
Move on.

So I looked behind me,
Stared it straight in the eyes.
I smiled as it caught me,
But not by surprise.

I let it carry me
To and fro,
Beyond limitation,
Beyond my shadow.

It rushed through my body,
It tossed me up and down.
I loved the storms glow,
Like it was renowned.

Still he stood,
Marching forward,

Fearless like the sun.
The leader of his own
Marching band of one.

The Dream Queen

So much excitement in the room,
It was surreal like a lollipop for the driven.

The way she hugged me,
I could have found myself in heaven—
Or in oblivion.

"Turn me this way," she said.
"Turn me that way." It didn't matter.

The soft, sweet sound of wonder,
The golden hair that swept the floor.

I smelled her tears,
I felt her laughter.
It was like paradise only when she was near.

Too much wine?
Never.

Too many smiles?
How could that ever be true?

The soft, silky sweetness
Of the ever after
Crept into me through her,
My muse.

Brother Sun, Sister Moon

It's loud outside.
There are people,
So many of them.
They are talking,
Walking loudly.
Stalking the day,
Hunting the night.

Where are you?
Sleeping it all off,
Like dreams
Are better than reality.
Like sleepy eyes
Can tell me more
Than the world
In uproar
Could ever convey.

How dare I come
To wake you
Out of your slumber?
To pull you back
Into the noise
And confusion?
Into the panic
And delusion

Of another day?
Where the fake
Light shines
And the sun,
Seemingly real,
Sets—and only
When it sets
Can we feel
The heat of
The sun
Alive again.

Come with me,
My brother.
How selfish
Of me to ask
You to wake
From your dream.

Come with me,
My brother,
And walk
With me
Down the roads
Of lies
And truths forbidden.
When I am
With you,

I know I am
Safe from all
Of the storm.

Will you resent me,
My brother?
For pulling
You away from
Your slumber,
Back into the crowds
That speak
Like whispers of magic
That never
Come to life?

Will you ache
If I wake you
Once again
And remind
You of the pain
And the suffering
Of time?
The time before
You dreamed
Your dreams
All day,
All night,
Long?

Wrestle a little,
Rustle a little.
I am here,
My sister.
I will walk
With you
Through the storms
Of lies
And fake people,
In the storms
Of day
And night.

I will walk
With you
Into the sun
And in the rain
Until time
Passes us by,
If only for us
In a dream.

Passionate Lovers

But it's only one stop away.
Why can't you think of me?

But it's right here on our way.
Why won't you listen to me?

My patience is curbing downwards, deep.
Why won't you just stop and see me?

You keep saying it can wait.
Why do you only care about you first?

Here, it's right here, again, here.
You finally stopped to look and see?

Throw a shoe at your face,
Cringe in disgrace.
Still I love your face.
Our deep passionate love,
I can never erase.
What else could fit this place?
Where passion and love exist
In this place of rage and anger,
Hunger and twists and turns,
Of compromise and trial,
Of love and of denial.

Siren

Sing to me
Your song.
Love the poison,
Love the venom,
Biting me,
Deepening the scars,
Christening my head
Like a child.
Pour the venom
Deeper and deeper still,
Until the blood
Rushes to my head.
Until I can only see
The truth
Of what is ahead.
Venomous sniper,
Fangs of death,
You kiss me so
Softly against
My breast.
You make me feel
Alive until I bleed.
All I desire
Is the dream
Of these
Moments where

I am away
In your venomous
Stare, awake
But sleeping,
Sleeping but
Aware.
Take me away,
Serpent of the night.
Take me to heaven,
Free from fright.
Take me
With your poison
Leaking into me,
Blood rushing
Through my veins.
Fangs of delight,
Fangs of shame,
Take me away.
Remind me
Of who I am,
Venom of pain.
You bring me joy.
My heart longs
For you
Every moment
Of every day.
You shield me
As I adapt

To you.
You take me in;
It's all you can do.
Wrap me up,
Let me see
The light
Of my tomb,
Regenerated now
By the poison
You dreamed of
In me now.
No death
Can take me
Away from you.
My death
In you is my life
Again.
The pain
Will take me away.

Beads on Breasts

Beaded strings
Lay tight against my breasts,
Keeping them in,
Holding them tight.
I love the way I feel,
Turning myself on
In this strange circumstance
Where they will soon see it all.

I crave for them to know me.
I want them to touch me.
But a sacred fear lies in me.

If I give them all they see,
Transparent and without doubt,
Will they devour all of me?
All that I am laid barren,
Laid waste in their mouths,
Left alone.

Once there is nothing
More to devour,
They quench their thirst.
But, will I be satisfied?
Or should I hold still,
My beaded gown

Against my breasts,
Longing for my eyes alone
To see the beauty I am,
And to devour myself,
Warm in my eyes,
Once and for all?

Raging Love

I cringe next to you,
Lingering in fear

While I dream of you,
Warm against my breast,
Soft tongue in my mouth.

"Help me," I pray to you.
"I have been desperately
In love for so long."

"But, the tide is coming
And what you did
Will wash ashore."
I crave to forget.
I crave to crave you
So powerfully
That everything you are
Will make us forget.
I want you to forget too.
I want to erase
What the tide will
Wash in.

I want to wrap myself
In your essence.

I am tired and tried
From trying to decipher why.

Can't I just die here
In your arms,
Wasted away by our love?

The tide washed the rage
In from the quaking shore.
It washed into my eyes
Where I see your reflection
Quiver in the stormy waves,
Washing back to us
All those memories.

"But, I am dying to love you."
I cringe again,
Wasted away, emotive
And in love.

Wasted away,
Barely breathing,
Contemplating which death
Will be worse...
The death in your arms?
Or the death apart
From the beat I feel
In your heart?

My heart quakes.
I beg the tide to disappear.

"Please, just this once,
Disappear.
Go away.
Let me love you,
Oh, rage of stone.
In my eyes
That are your eyes,
Let the waves come
Ashore no more."

But, the quaking
Won't cease.

I cradle my breasts
In your arms,
My soul touching
Your stomach,
Remembering where
The fire came from—
Where the rage
Will live to see tomorrow.

Oh, can't it see
Darkness forever more?

Rage in the sun,
My love.
Rage in my heart,
My soul.
Rage in my body,
Feel my life.
Know that I loved
You then,
I will love you now,
I will rage with you,
Until tomorrow's sun
Brings the tide in
Once again to shore,
With only our love
Where we rage together,
In love,
Against the quaking storm.

Easy Death

My eyes sad and weeping.

How easy this is for you,
To take the knife and dig it
Into my skin,
Piercing my heart,
Driving deep,
Cutting bones,
Stealing the air
From my lungs,
Cutting open my chest,
Plunging deep into my heart
Again
And again
And again.
So many slices,
My body
Cut open like a cake.
Blood the filling,
Oozing
Out of my skin.
My eyes tired, weeping,
Closing shut,
Off to a dreamless sleep.
In the darkness
The pain slips away

Into my conscious,
Severed from my flesh.
Torn away
From my broken body.
How easy is it for you
To see me weep,
As the long, dark night
Holds my hand
And crosses me over.

The Reacher

My body said no.

My body said wait!

But the arms kept crossing
That uncrossable place.

I felt my heart,
My lungs,
My body,
Melt into the pull.

I resisted
With all my heart,
Energy, and soul.

The reacher...

Kept crawling

Under my skin,
In my body.

Until...

I could only
Come to reach

For the reacher too.

All that was left
Was the reacher,

And my heart
Reaching, too.

The Child's Play

My head lost
In my hands,

Me laughing,
Me squirming.

My head
In my hands,

Me remembering
Funny things,
Laughing at
All the things.

The things
That gave me
Smiles,
Giggles,
Laughs.

My head
In my hands,

Severed from
My body
In bliss,

Coming forward.

My head
In my hands,

Them laughing.
My stitches
So loud,
Visible,
Running
Through
My neck.

My head
In my hands,

There they stood,
Wishing
They could
Be like me.

My head
In my hands,

After all.

My head
In my hands.

Magic

Cheater?!
Who?
Me?!

But it was love.
I swear it.
It was magic.
Yes!
But, it was still love.

Why do you stare
At me,
Like I cheated?
Like my magic
Is evil,
Full of lies?

Why do you deny it?!
It was my power.
It was my heart.
It was my choice.
It was my life.

Magic?
Yes, it was.
But, it was still love.

The Girl Who Cried

Staring out of the window,
That face, still in his fancy car,
With his muscles protruding from his shirt,
Too tight on his body,
Like his tight, ugly expression.
Growling
Like nothing could make him afraid,
Like only he could do the harming.
Taking the power all for himself.
She, weeping at his mercy,
Too tired to imagine tomorrow,
Too exhausted to wonder,
When he would be back again.
Pain by the windowpane,
Tears shed within instead of without,
Tears wept in silence,
Eyes swollen with fear,
And a tearless fright she wished
She would never face again.

The Vampire

"Why won't you kiss me?"
he asked, demanding his will.
The younger one,
So much sweeter to the eyes
And flavorful to the tongue.
But, the elder one,
The one stricken with age
And strange breath,
Fought hard for those lips,
Red and soft.
"Kiss me! Why do you resist?"
Her eyes on the younger one,
Tasting never felt so sweet.
His lips approaching her,
Fighting her resistance.
Tonight! You will see
My taste is just as sweet.
He pushed his mouth hard
Against her lips
Until her mouth drowned,
Overtaken by his will
And lips that tasted
Sugary sweet.

The Gifted One

Let no one find me.
I am hiding,
Hiding from you,
Obscure and Difficult One.
You shine with your eyes
Glittering like the sun,
But your core is dark
Like gray skies.
Like Armageddon.
Like death
Disguised as life.
Here I am,
Sitting at the window,
Eating my porridge,
Gray and bleak.
Like the sound
Of your footsteps
Coming for me,
Walking closer,
Captivating my breath
And leaving me
Speechless, my heart
Broken and alone.
You saw my gift,
Then you broke me,
Crippled me,

Made me again
Into nothing,
Into no one,
So obscured
In judgment,
In life itself.
I crawl away,
I long to run,
But there are your eyes
Shining like the sun.
Darkened by the moon,
Reminding me
Why I prefer
The shadow.
Leaping large
And caressing my brain,
Awakening me
Once again
To the absence
Of you.
Soul of mine,
Love of life,
Bringer of death,
Keeper of logic,
Defiler of the faith,
Runner of minds,
Weakened as the will
Of us is

Longing for truth
While all we are fed
Are lies.
Come to me.
May I be your gifted one?
Stronger than life,
Bigger than the sun?

Half and Half

Half me,
Half you,
Half animal,
Half lust.
I saw
The mermaid,
The half man,
The half woman,
The half fish.
The mud
Underneath me,
Underneath us.
Arms intertwined,
Love obvious,
The man,
The woman,
And the fish
Combined
In the dirty,
Muddy waters
Of our messy,
Wet lives.

moments in
SLUMBER